CONVERSATIONS WITH

THOMAS PAINE

THE FOUNDING FATHER

WITHOUT A GRAVE

BOOK 1

ISBN-10: 1491230975
ISBN-13: 978-1491230978

----DEDICATION----

This writing is dedicated to Thomas Paine, Father of American Democracy and Father of the American Revolution, whose ideas and writings inspired those who came before us to form the United States of America based on the unique principle of power flowing from the people to the Government.

It seems only logical that when evaluating our Democracy that we should return to Mr. Paine, whose idea it was in the first place, to seek his guidance related to maintaining, keeping, and earning the return of our Democracy.

INTRODUCTION

Thomas Paine is the Founding Father of American Democracy and is without a grave. His body was left in a trunk in an attic. Some of his bones became buttons, while the rest were scattered to places yet unknown. These actions are cheered by many Christian leaders worldwide to this day as being sound Christian punishment.

Question: If the United States of America no longer follows the writings of the Father of American Democracy, then is the United States still a Democracy?

Mr. Paine's writings were well received and inspired the suppressed people of the American Colonies to stand against tyranny and fight for our freedom. Thomas Paine stood up for the American people before we were known as the American people. He secured benefits and rights for people that are being lost and taken for granted today and for which he paid dearly. The individual rights he spoke of are mostly being manipulated away from us. He is the father of American Democracy but was denied its benefits by a supposedly Christian society and became Democracy's first martyr. His life stands as an example that America was never really a Christian nation.

Many of the Founding Fathers agreed with Thomas Paine, not only regarding his democratic governmental views, but also his views regarding man-made organized religions:

The United States is in no way founded upon the Christian religion.
---- George Washington and John Adams.

This would be the best of all possible worlds, if there were no religion at all.
---- John Adams: Letter to Thomas Jefferson.

In every country and in every age, the priest has been hostile to liberty. He is always in alliance with the despot, abetting his abuses in return for protection to his own.
---- Thomas Jefferson.

I do not find in orthodox Christianity one redeeming feature.
----Thomas Jefferson.

And of course from the individual, who more than any other, carried forward the flag of Democracy raised by the Founding Fathers:

The Bible is not my book, and Christianity is not my religion. I could never give assent to the long complicated statements of Christian dogma.
---- Abraham Lincoln.

The major difference between Thomas Paine and the rest of the Founding Fathers is that Thomas Paine actually published an entire book about the abuses of religious leaders and man-made organized religion in general called the Age of Reason. He was not against people believing in and practicing their various religions. In point of fact, Mr. Paine believed very deeply in God. Mr. Paine championed Freedom of religion, but he also stood staunchly against how religious leaders represented God here on earth and how they used God to abuse everyday people. Freedom of Religion is not just for Christians but protects the right of all people to worship God without interference and without interfering with the religious beliefs of others, and that is all.

Mr. Paine believed deeply in God, but he also believed that religious organizations historically usurping ownership of the various religions to represent God, are mostly dedicated to the acquisition of profits, real estate, personal power, political power and not representative of God at all; thus resulting in the removal of God from religion, the abuse of millions of people worldwide, and a Right Wing danger to Democracy.

He was denied Freedom of speech, Freedom of religion, and just about every Freedom the new Constitution provided. He was hounded on his death bed by Christian leaders to recant his writings against them and man-made organized religion. Mr. Paine refused to deny his beliefs regarding the abuses of man-made religions to his last breath and his bones were eventually dug up and lost or scattered as punishment. The severe reaction of Christian leaders against him suggests that Thomas Paine came extremely close to the truth regarding the abuses of man-made organized religion. Mr. Paine was not a summer soldier nor a sunshine patriot. He stood by, and for, his word and writings to the death.

However, before his body was dug up and desecrated, he did have a funeral. In attendance were, Mme. De Bonneville, who took care of Mr. Paine during the last leg of his journey toward death, her two sons, one of whom became a well-regarded Union Civil War General; Willett Hicks, a Quaker Preacher who remained his staunch friend at great risk to his earthly Christianity, and two slaves who reportedly walked twenty-two miles to honor the only man of his color with enough courage to write, speak publically, and stand for Black Equality. Only six people mustered up for the funeral of the man who was the Father of the American Revolution and whose ideas and writings spawned our American Democracy. The seeds of Democracy were well sown and Mr. Paine's life was indeed well spent.

Mr. Paine has also been credited with being the father of the American Revolution. His writings inspired America's first 'Greatest Generation' to stand together and fight the long fight to win their Freedom and use Mr. Paine's new ideas about Government by the people to develop an American Democracy that has never since been duplicated and is currently being put to the sword by the Right Wing of the Republican Party.

He actually believed that everyday people on the entire planet had individual rights and if they somehow stood up as one, they could even keep those individual rights for themselves and their children. Protecting the beliefs and accomplishments of Thomas Paine, made on behalf of the American people past, present, and future, is the greatest challenge Democracy in America faces today.

Thomas Paine believed that each of us has a right to express our opinion and speak freely, as eventually was spoken in the Constitution. This he was denied. Yet who more than any other should have this right respected. After all, this experiment called American Democracy was his idea.

Pick your Government and support it:
 --- Alexander Hamilton.

Without the pen of the Author of Common Sense, the sword of Washington would have been raised in vain:
---- John Adams.

History is to ascribe the American Revolution to Thomas Paine:
---- John Adams.

The citizens of the United States cannot look upon the time of their own revolution without

recollecting among the names of their most distinguished patriots, that of Thomas Paine:
---- James Monroe.

America is indebted to few characters more than you: (Thomas Paine)
---- Gen. Nathaniel Greene.

Free America without Thomas Paine is unthinkable:
---- Lafayette.

And following that vein down through the years: Good intentions will always be pleaded for every assumption of authority. It is hardly too strong to say that the Constitution was made to guard the people against the dangers of good intentions. There are men in all ages who mean to govern well, but they mean to govern. They promise to be good masters, but they mean to be masters:
---- Daniel Webster.

Those who make peaceful revolution impossible will make violent revolution inevitable:
---- John F. Kennedy.

Beware of the Military-Industrial complex.
---- Dwight Eisenhower.

The difference between death and taxes is death doesn't get worse every time Congress meets:
---- Will Rogers.

Government of the people, by the people, for the people:
---- Abraham Lincoln

Conversations with Thomas Paine

Chapter One: Our First Meeting.

Did you ever have a night where no matter what you did or whatever remedy you attempted, sleep just refused to have anything to do with you?

Not so long ago, I had one of those nights. The house was dark and I was wide awake and too restless to work or read.

So, I gave into the situation, brewed a pot of strong coffee and stepped onto the small porch adjacent to the sunroom to see what the night would provide.

I sat down to enjoy the rising moon that cast a wide bright silvery path across the bay leading directly to our old cape style house. The night view looking across the old rural coast road that runs along the entire New England Coast was, as always, magnificent and relaxing.

I would sometimes try to imagine what the old coast road was like during the Revolutionary War period; citizen soldiers moving back and forth past this very spot on their way to the various cities, hamlets, battlefields of that time, attending gatherings and trying to learn how to build a brand new type of nation. A nation founded on the unheard concept of freedom for all, with power flowing from the people to the government; people making the laws, becoming Presidents, Congressmen, and Judges back when people actually went into government to protect the rights of their neighbors and really tried to represent the people. But then again, the generation of the Founding Fathers were not just soldiers, politicians, bankers, and businessmen living by today's self-centered standards; they became much more.

This house, this porch, and all the families that have dwelled here have been a living history of the passage of American generations moving up and back along the road to protect and continually build and adjust America's experiment in freedom and democracy. And they have protected and maintained it very well indeed till this generation.

Many Americans who went down that road never returned home. We try to keep faith with them by etching their names on large stone obelisks erected in prominent places in town squares with chiseled words that stand as tributes to their bravery, sacrifice, and of their lives cut short. Don't know if that's enough, but it's all we have.

As I held the warm cup with both hands, sipping oh so quietly and breathing in the mild aroma of freshly brewed coffee, I began to notice differences about my usually predictable surroundings that set this night apart from the many other nights.

I saw trees gently swaying at the touch of a gentle breeze, and yet I felt no breeze.

The moon, although bright and silvery, had a slight reddish yellow cast to it circled by a moisture ring of mild multiple colors.

And there was not a sound to be heard. No usual critters scurrying past. No Moose crossing the road. No night birds or loons at all. Not even a cricket or creak of the house could be heard.

Everything was so quiet and still that I was forced to shallow breathing just out of respect.

My observations were interrupted by a movement off to my right.

I saw a man walking up the road who, by the measure of his gait, seemed to be deep in thought or contemplation.

He was of good stature and wearing some kind of costume. I reasoned that he may have joined in the festivities earlier in the evening and was steadying his steps for the journey home, possibly having a bit more drink than originally planned.

He stopped along the road in front of our porch with his back to me and was enjoying the same night view as myself.

Ahoy stranger, I have an extra chair and cup if you would like to rest awhile before continuing your journey.

I then wondered why I had brought an extra cup onto the porch.

He turned in my direction. With the moon at his back I could distinguish no features. He looked like a shadow silhouetted against the rising moon.

He began to walk toward the porch removing his three pointed hat.

Thank you neighbor, I believe I will accept your kindness for I am quite weary and have a long journey yet ahead of me.

He stepped onto the porch, shook my hand, and sat down across from me while I poured him a good cup of the favored coffee.

He sat back, stretched out his legs, held the warm cup with both hands, sighed and drank a good measure.

This is really a good draft. You wouldn't happen to have some spirits to add to this fine taste, would you neighbor?

I believe I may have a drop or two about the place, I replied.
When I returned, I placed the bottle on the table.

He thanked me and added a small measure to his coffee and to mine.

We both sat back and enjoyed the silence and the view for some time.

What happened??

I had just started to drift off when I heard his question and really didn't know what he meant.

Sorry, you have the better of me sir.
What happened to what?

I reached over and poured him and myself a bit more coffee while he in turn added a bit more spirit to our drinks.

Government is supposed to receive their power from the citizens that elect them to office and act accordingly on behalf of those people. During my travels along this road I have observed that the flow of power has reversed. Government now dictates to the people.
It grieves me greatly to see this, so I ask again neighbor; what happened?

That is quite a question sir. Your comment is quite true and I believe that any answer that I offer would sound like a series of pathetic excuses. I do not believe that the people know what to do about it.

I could say that times have changed and people have changed. The times have changed but people haven't, while the Constitution has been discarded.

I could say that the political pendulum swinging left and right, this time, on its journey right, swung right through the back door of the Republican Party and burst into Fascism just as it could have broken through the back door of the Democratic Party and burst into Communism had it been traveling left.

You are right neighbor, the Constitution has been discarded and your answers are well likened to pathetic excuses. And yes, the times have changed but I disagree that people have not changed. The People have changed most decidedly.

In my travels neighbor, I hear no public debate about independence or freedom. Not even a whisper of what was once so primary. People discussing freedom and how, and who, to elect to keep freedom of the people is the cornerstone of our democracy. The interchange of ideas about keeping all involved and learning freedom have always been traditional conversation within families, homes, workplaces, schools, and public meeting places.

This great nation, built with great individual sacrifice by the people, is no longer a Republic. Its flag no longer symbolizes Freedom and Democracy.

Yes, I believe you are correct Mr. Paine. However, I am beginning to hear these types of conversations. Not many, but people are beginning to notice that many of the rights granted by the Constitution have disappeared and have been replaced with anti individual rights administrative law courts, and Right Wing Christian Fascism hiding in altered religion; altered by the removal of God.

Well neighbor, even during my time man had, centuries previous, already removed the presence of God from all religions, and had replaced God with abuse of people and quests for power and profits. Religion is this planet's oldest business corporation.

But now a question: What are these Administrative law courts you mention neighbor? I don't recall anything about such courts in the Constitution of these United States. I'd like to hear more about this neighbor at a later time, but for now; how really stands the Constitution?

Discarded, dusty, and neglected, Mr. Paine; rarely taught in schools anymore.

Mr. Paine sat back, sipped his drink and spoke words that I hadn't heard or read in many years from his Crisis Pamphlet Series.

These are the times that try men's souls: The summer soldier and sunshine patriot will, in this crisis, shrink from the service of their country; but he that stands it now, deserves the love and thanks of man and woman. Tyranny, like hell, is not easily conquered; yet we have this consolation with us, that the harder the conflict, the more glorious the triumph. What we obtain too cheap, we esteem too lightly; it is dearness that gives everything its value. Heaven knows how to put a proper price upon its goods; and it would be strange indeed if so celestial an article as Freedom should not be highly rated.

Great inspirational words Mr. Paine. Some say that you wrote them at Valley Forge on the back of drum?

Yes, on the back of a drum, but no neighbor, not at Valley Forge. I wrote this first Crisis Pamphlet in December, 1776. We retreated into winter quarters at Valley Forge in December, 1777. This first pamphlet, and others, did find use that winter while rebuilding our Army, if we could be called an Army at that time having just suffered two defeats.

Mr. Paine sat back, took a sip of coffee and spirits and asked.
Do my words that General Washington chose to read to our soldiers prior to crossing the Delaware and defeating the Hessians at Trenton on Christmas day, 1776, and later the British at Princeton even apply these days neighbor?

My embarrassment had no answer for him, so I simply replied: Your words still apply quite strongly and may yet again be applied when people of today begin to notice that their freedom is being usurped by the so called Christian Fascist Right.

With a heavy sigh, Mr. Paine finished his spirited coffee and indicated that he needed to continue his journey but further remarked: Yes, of course, those Pharisees, the usurpers of individual freedom have raised the beasts ugly head cloaked in religion yet again, and once more impose slavery where representation of the people is guaranteed and required.

He thanked me, shook my hand and asked if he could soon return to continue our conversation.

I told him that I would keep the coffee fresh and the bottle full.

I watched as Mr. Paine walked down the road disappearing completely into the darkness.

I sat down, reached for my cup and contemplated our first conversation.

I felt a soft cool breeze gently move across my cheek and listened to the now again present night sounds till first light.

Conversations with Thomas Paine

Chapter Two: The Loss of Free Will.

Sometime had elapsed since Mr. Paine stopped by for a chat. I had decided that the whole episode had been nothing more than a dream; a very intense good welcomed dream, but just a dream. The dream had seemed so real and memorable. Nothing to do but carry on with the wonders of everyday life till a possible next meeting, or not. Brass it out as we said when we were young.

This thought moved me to do something that I had never done before as the evening moved forward ever so slowly toward moonrise. I walked the entire length of the cape house repeatedly; starting at the sunroom through what we call the blueberry room, across the hall to the dining room, then kitchen, and roaster area. Back and forth, hour after hour till I looked out the dining room window and saw the reddish yellow hue of the moon rising from the bay's horizon.

I ground some freshly roasted coffee beans and brewed a pot of coffee, grabbed two mugs, and of course the spirited bottle and stepped again onto the porch adjacent the sunroom. I thought it only good manners to wait till my guest arrived before commencing the coffee mess.

The chair was quite comfortable so I stretched out and took in the silvery view and readied myself to enjoy the silence and the conversation that would follow. However, something was different. My customary surroundings remained customary by not going silent. Critters, crickets, birds, and loons continued to serenade the night. There was no movement or hint of anyone traveling up or down the old coast road.

The night offered no chance for disappointment due to the fact that I fell fast asleep. The soft touch of a hand to my shoulder brought me wide awake without startle.

Greetings neighbor, the thought of your fine coffee and spirits have sustained me throughout my travels.

I stretched and yawned as Mr. Paine sat opposite and poured us both coffee, and this time, a sound measure of spirits. I thanked him, took the mug in both hands, breathed in the refreshing aroma, as did he, and we both sat back quietly looking out across the coast road, enjoying the return of complete silence and the wide silvery path laying invitingly on the still water.

We sat in silence for what I thought to be a long time before looking over at him to see if he had fallen asleep. He looked back and indicated that he thought I had gone back to my dreams. We both laughed and refreshed our cups.

You look as though something is troubling you neighbor.

Yes, I have been wondering if you are really here or if I am here alone having a conversation with myself.

Was it not the touch of my hand that woke you? Besides, if I were not present you would not see me.

Good points Mr. Paine. What would you like to talk about this evening?

I have been studying this Administrative Law item that you mentioned last time neighbor and my impression is that it is a separate court or legal system that takes away the individual rights set forth in the Constitution that are specifically reserved for individual citizens, and gives them to non-human entities such as companies, government agencies, insurance speculators, utility companies, school districts and the like. Administrative Law operates totally outside the Constitution.

Companies, governments, and individuals cannot contract or legislate around the Constitution as is currently being done. These non-human corporate entities become the defendant, usurping defendant protections in court proceedings. The individual, victimized by these entities, is forced into becoming the prosecutor thus losing the individual right of due process given to him by the Constitution. The individual victim also loses all right to counsel. Counsel is not guaranteed under Administrative Law and will not be provided for the individual victim. Now, corporations are people? And not good people.

I have never witnessed anything so obviously and blatantly unconstitutional and anti-democracy. It troubles me greatly because it further allows power to flow from government to the people instead of from the people to the government as originally intended and written, thus demonstrating that government here in your time is no longer a democracy. The Supreme Court of the United States must have somehow been nullified or cancelled as the third branch of government for this to have happened. I suspect a complete absence of integrity and the meddling in government by churches. Wherever did this Administrative Law abomination come from neighbor?

Mostly from a combination of Nazi Germany and an outgrowth of our own popular Fascist movement during the 1920's and 30's. Germany called their illegal courts Special Courts or People's Courts, while in America we call them Administrative Law Courts. Both are designed to remove individual rights and take away property and all judicial recourse from the people. Fascism attacks and begins the destruction of Democracy by altering or changing Democracy's court system at the local, state and federal levels, and especially concentrates on the Supreme Court of these United States.

Neighbor, how did you form this opinion about administrative law? Are you in the legal profession?

No, Mr. Paine I am not part of the legal profession. I'm just an individual who once lived in a prosperous democracy and remembers what is was like and is currently searching for ways to get it back. There are corrupt right wing business leaders, politicians, judges, educators, and many others that carry their bias against people far to the Right beyond the boundaries of Democracy and into the killing fields of Fascism. The effect is the fostering of personal hatred and bias in common everyday dealings which gradually kills Democracy whether intentional or not. This negative situation is maintained by extreme right wing attorneys protecting extreme right wing factions by finding illegal ways around federal, state, and local laws and regulations, thus becoming the shovels that bury Democracy. In other words, the contracting around the United States Constitution, all State Constitutions and local community councils in general.

Let me also inquire about the democracy that you recall from your distant youth neighbor. Was that prosperous democracy a democracy that included all people?

Well Mr. Paine, I cannot say that it was. There existed, inequality of income, racism, and discrimination, as there always have been in

America, but I believe that these things existed in lesser amounts, during my 'distant youth' era, than they do here in our time and for our conversations here in the present.

Do not forget neighbor that the rise of right wing Fascism and associated inequality and suppression is not the first occurrence of that evil here in America.

Yes Mr. Paine, it does appear that the beast has returned.

As you form your opinions neighbor, you should be aware that we, you call the Founding Fathers had many disagreements and numbers of discussions regarding all manner of positions about how and for whom a democracy should function. However, on one item, there appeared to be universal agreement among us. That item is income inequality. It was felt that income inequality alone could lead to the downfall of our new democracy, or any government for that matter. We, the Founding Fathers, came from Christian Europe where income inequality formed the basis for all types of inequality for many centuries as slaves of conquerors, serfs to landowners of the feudal system, as oppressed people of monarchies, and later as slaves, tenant farmers, and migrant workers here in America. Based on our violent world history of suppression alone I wrote that our democracy should provide a guaranteed income for all the people; an income that would provide for basic needs and avoid the development of all types of tyranny that develop when small groups or 'divine right' families usurp the money and power of a nation. Leaders of your time have neglected this in the extreme which has led to what you now call gridlock and that I call gridlock of democracy for the people.

Are you saying Mr. Paine that inequality, especially income inequality is the rock upon which the foundations of Right Wing and Left Wing policies are built against people and form Communism and Fascism in general, while income equality through guaranteed income allows money to continually circulate through the economy thus not allowing the economy to drop into suppression of the people thereby maintaining democracy?

Exactly neighbor, well struck; protection of the individual's economy as the rock of democracy leading to the stabilization of life, thus protecting democracy from being usurped by the tyranny of both extremes, especially the Christian right and corporate corruption in general.

Apologies if I may have digressed neighbor, because for a moment there, it appeared to me that you were straying into the wrong meadow and away from the needed specifics, please proceed with your opinion about this unconstitutional administrative law abomination while I pour more of this fine draft. Remember though as you continue, that the people in general must want to live free as a Democracy and accept the responsibility, and nay say the hardships of protecting our still young Democracy.

My opinion is based on the words of President Franklin Delano Roosevelt, Mr. Paine, who commissioned a report as early as 1939 while fascist supporters in both political parties of our declining democracy were lobbying for United States involvement supporting Hitler.

Mr. Roosevelt indicated that the practice of creating administrative agencies with the authority to perform both legislative and judicial duties 'threatens to develop a fourth branch of government for which there is no sanction in the Constitution.'

You see Mr. Paine, I believe that words such as these from the President who developed New Deal programs to rebuild our infrastructure to bring us successfully through the Great Depression and then stepped up to become the leader of the Greatest Generation that fought and won World War Two are words given to the people to use to protect our freedom and Democracy.

Besides, if FDR believed that administrative law was unconstitutional, then that, sir, is good enough for me.

It appears to me that such words and New Deal programs are needed in the United States again. I am in full agreement with you neighbor. But, how is it then that administrative law so prevalent a cancer infecting our judicial system toward a governmental change from Democracy to Fascism is so widely in place at the local, state and federal levels of society here in your time if it was adjudged as being unconstitutional by one of our greatest Presidents more than seventy of your years ago?

I was ready to discuss the 1946 Administrative Procedure Act, the seed of this judicial cancer, passed by the Fascist factions of both parties, within Congress even before all the troops of the

Greatest Generation were yet home from defeating Fascism and provide cases clearly demonstrating that Administrative Law usurps our individual rights, and show it's connection to Republican Right Wing corruption when Mr. Paine indicated that Administrative Law perverting the Constitution was not what he came to discuss this evening. He wanted to discuss the perverse cause that led to the loss of Constitutional individual rights and the setting up of this separate illegal judicial system; man-made organized religion.

I could not have been more surprised.

Are you speaking about your writing in the Age of Reason, Mr. Paine?
Do you see a connection between current Administrative Law and leaders who design man-made religion?

There are times when I wish I had never written Age of Reason. Mr. Franklin warned me vigorously regarding publishing the discourse. Lost just about all of my friends and made a lot more enemies than was reasonable.
Yes, Administrative Law appears to be an outgrowth of the same flawed religious thinking responsible for separating God from religion and

replacing him with corrupt business practices and abuse. If abuse in religion is allowed, can governmental change to tyranny be far behind, neighbor?

Many Americans, neighbor, seem to have forgotten that a great many people that fought the Revolution and built these United States did so because they were victims of religious persecution in their home countries in Europe. They wanted to live in a nation where all people could live free and worship God in whatever way they wished without religious abuse and without disruption from other religions. Governments controlled by organized man-made religions are dictatorships and force tyranny upon the people. God did not want people to organize religion into the largest business in the world and control governments, to declare war on other nations and kill people in order to convert them to their way of worshipping God. Why, the Thirty Years War alone killed twenty per cent of the entire population of Germany. The many Crusades, the Inquisition, Catholic priests abusing children, scandal after scandal of your evangelicals on television, Muslims declaring religious wars, are all examples of religious corruption of which God cannot, and will not be a part. God is actually trying to show us that people are their own church and to stop man-made religion from killing and abusing people in his name.

In other words, keep God in your hearts and man-made perverted religion, no matter what name is used, out of government. I believe that so called religions that take over governments and declare wars can no longer be termed religions and must be fought and defeated like any hostile bigoted aggressive nation, as was done in World War II. To win such a war, all the dogs must be loosed.

You see neighbor, the families of the founding fathers fled Europe because of religious persecution. What people today don't realize is that we were fleeing from other Christians. Christians killing Christians was the norm. That is why separation of church and state was placed so strongly in the Constitution. We knew first hand that the organizational structure of any religion was open to the corruption and abuse of big business and that future generations would always have people who aspired to power through tyranny, dictatorship, and monarchy by using religion falsely, just as in our time. They could be likened to false Christians. Beware of false prophets, remember?

It was James Madison, neighbor, who pointed out that the purpose of separation of church and state is to keep forever from these shores the ceaseless strife that has soaked the soil of Europe in blood. He was well applauded for those words.

Mr. Madison would not be applauded by the republicans of today. In our time Mr. Paine, we call such abuse the Tea Party movement, representing America's own Brown Shirts. The march to Fascism through intimidation and violence mirroring Germany of the twenties and thirties and the German American Bund of the same period which tried to establish a strong foothold for Hitler here in America. It almost worked. Hitler was very popular, especially with politicians, bankers, and business leaders here in America during our time called the Great Depression.
Didn't your friend and sponsor, Benjamin Franklin, have something to say about religion Mr. Paine?

He surely did neighbor. I recall Mr. Franklin telling me that when a religion is good, I conceive it will support itself and when it does not support itself, and God does not care to support it so that it's professionals are obliged to call for the help of civil power 'tis a sign, he apprehended of its being a bad one. I believe that Mr. Franklin also said that lighthouses are more helpful than churches and that early in life he absented himself from Christian assemblies. He is a good and wise friend.

Overall Mr. Paine, it sounds like many people in your time were influenced by the Deism movement; arriving at the existence of God through reason and observation of nature instead of biblical stories of miracles, floods, pestilence, and punishment. I think you also mean that when a political section of a religion, like the extreme right wing declares war, they declare war in the name of the entire population of the religion no matter how many governments they control or where they live. Governments are responsible for all the activities that are conducted within their own borders.

That's right neighbor, partially Deism. However, the entire religious nation or any nation that declares war for whatever reason must be defeated and its entire population be subjected to the effects of total war, as is currently being done to the people of the United States today. Besides, did you really believe what you were told in school that you would go to hell if you missed church on Sunday? And by the way, if today's tea party people were alive during the Revolutionary War, they would be called Tories supporting King George and fighting against the Founding Fathers and the new Democracy. The Boston Tea Party Americans would have enthusiastically tossed your current Tea Party people into Boston Harbor and the crates of the Kings tea in on top of them.

I must admit, Mr. Paine, that at first I did believe that I would go to hell by missing church on Sunday. Soon though, I noticed that church services and sermons were more about collecting money and less about God.

Exactly neighbor, Jesus never wrote anything in his own hand and I take that as a sign. All religion is man-made and subject to the individual bias possessed by the writers of the various religious texts and all is hearsay. God bestowed free will upon us and does not interfere in the daily lives of individuals and their journey through life. Each individual is their own church. Believing in God without notions of supernatural revelation as a basis of truth or religious dogma put many of our time in direct contrast to Christian, Islamic, and Judaic teachings. It was unusual, to say the least, for

Christians to believe that people arrive at religious truths through reason and observations of the natural world.

Neighbor, I believe that God bestowed upon each individual that ever lived or ever will live the gift of free will. It is the responsibility of each individual to decide what to do with that free will. God gave us free will and would not step in when we move in a negative direction, otherwise free will would not be free will. Democracy provides the protection for our God given free will, but Democracy must be jealously protected and understood by the people. Democracy, like free will, can be lost, given, or taken away as is now happening here in your time.

I agree Mr. Paine. I believe that the lesson here is that God wanted people to realize that each individual is the church of which he spoke and to avoid the idea of organized religion because man-made organizational structures become business for the concentration of wealth and power for the benefit of a few. This in turn leads to bigotry, hatred, tyranny, abuse, war, killing, and the subjugation and removal of God endowed free will. You are correct Mr. Paine; religion as designed by man is dictatorship.

Religion as designed by God protects and fosters his greatest gift to us; free will which in turn is manifested through freedom and democracy.

Well spoken, neighbor, well spoken, but remember, the people voted the current Republican Party of Fascism into the Government and are choosing Fascism over Democracy. That is also free will.

Mr. Paine, voting against one's own Freedom would be absurd.

It has been done before neighbor.

When?

Germany, after World War One, during your Roaring Twenties, and the Great Depression. The bankers and corporations in America and England and other countries made fortunes building Hitler's Fascist war machine. I also believe that the last Apostle was not yet dead when men were using religion to attack and remove the free will of the people.

Here, here!

I reached over and refilled our cups with the spirited brew as we both sat back to contemplate the meanings of our conversation. I myself was a bit embarrassed by my outburst and I noticed that Mr. Paine wore a small smile.

What I view as one of the most amazing coincidences in history, Mr. Paine, is that these altered beliefs of religion peaked at about the time of the American Revolution and played a major role in creating the unheard of principle of separation of church and state, as expressed in Jefferson's letters and the principle of religious freedom as expressed in the first amendment of the United States Constitution.

Yes, and look at the people that Deism influenced neighbor; Washington, Jefferson, Adams, Franklin, Madison, Hamilton, Allen, plus thousands more as well as myself. Many of these people were politically direct opposites and fought, tussled, and argued with each other throughout their lifetimes. Why, Jefferson and Adams argued bitterly right to their death beds on July fourth, a full fifty years after the original fourth thus cementing democracy throughout the United States. I find that truly amazing.

I think, Mr. Paine, that it may be the only example of true bipartisanship in all of United States History.

We both laughed and expressed our agreement.

Additionally Mr. Paine, I know Deism proponents such as you, believe that God set things in motion at the beginning and then left us on our own to sort things out, but I must say that I see the hand of God giving us a nudge in the right direction sometime just before 1776. The effect was too great and world changing to have been simply coincidence. God must be greatly disappointed to see that the experiment has lasted only just a bit over two hundred years.

The battle is yet enjoined and the grapple continues ever more fiercely neighbor. The fight for freedom never ends and is especially difficult when the enemies are within the borders of our society and seek to change society and its people to their tyrannical bias or to break away and start yet another country controlled by dictatorship either based on religious beliefs or a state completely devoid of God. You see neighbor, freedom and democracy walk the middle road between these two great Left and Right evils while each extreme attempts every corrupt method possible to pull freedom, democracy, and free will into their respective lairs to impose slavery and destruction upon a population not paying attention. When, and if, the banner of America falls, another people somewhere will snatch it up and continue the fight. The protection of democracy and keeping it firmly on that middle road is a birth to death individual responsibility. Your schools and your population of today have forgotten this in the extreme.

There is great truth in your perspective Mr. Paine, unfortunately.

After a long silent interval, I went back into the house for more coffee. The brew had gone cold and a warning chill of impending danger had crept upon me. Upon my return I poured fresh cups while Mr. Paine added the spirits.

Mr. Paine, do you think that everyday people of your time were influenced by the temporary altering of Christian beliefs?

Why do you say temporary, neighbor?

Well, by 1800, Deism was already not as popular and was, unfortunately, developing into yet another abusive form of organized religion and also by the negative reactions to your writing of the Age of Reason. I believe that God did not want us to build a physical church upon the Rock of Peter. I believe God wanted us to use Peter as the model by which to live and that the church to which God refers would live in our souls and not be a building used to grow organized abuse and corruption. I believe the parts of Deism that influenced our Constitution were intended to be an idea to live by just as freedom and democracy are ideas that people should learn to live by in order to keep their freedom. I say temporary due to noting the abuse and religious wars for profit here in my time Mr. Paine.

Come to think of it neighbor, your republican party of today does closely resemble that building used to grow organized abuse and corruption that you mention. That's exactly why I wrote Age of Reason later in life. The ideas were fading, just as the ideas of Democracy are fading here in your time. The negative reaction to my writing at that time was a necessary but unwelcome personal surprise. The everyday person during the Revolution was greatly influenced by Christian belief alterations brought about by Deism.

If you don't mind the personal reference neighbor, I will try to describe what I saw in the faces of our soldiers while retreating on Valley Forge. I was first struck by their ages. There were boys as young as thirteen and men that had long past their sixtieth year, as well as all the ages between. There were differences in religion and color. But they all had a look about them, not so much while marching, but quite noticeable while sitting along roadsides and in hamlets. They had the look of both predator and prey; of determination and fear. I could tell by looking at them that no matter what hardship needed to be endured, they would never give up and that eventually we would win our freedom. I wondered at times if this trait would be uniquely American. I believe that it is uniquely American. Is it still so today?

Not as much as then, Mr. Paine, not as much. We have a good foundation of reserve citizen soldiers, volunteers all that are currently being overused and stretched quite thin fighting the war profiteering diversions designed to weaken us by our enemies from within and without. Abuse of military women and those men that help them, suicide, theft, fraud, and selling awards to friends, and altering records runs high. We also use mercenaries, highly paid from our tax dollars, employed by companies awarded government contracts through the efforts of our religious controlled Republican Right Wing.

Hold on neighbor. You mean like Hessian mercenaries used by King George against us during our war for independence?

Similar, but these mercenaries are citizens as well as some non-citizens employed by government contracted companies to provide security in war zones for highly ranked individuals, do intelligence work for the capture and torture of possible Islamic terrorists, and are highly paid from tax dollars.

Isn't what you call war zone security the job of the regular military? I am greatly disturbed by your descriptions. Mercenaries, torture, invasions, Christian government and, subjugation of individual rights are all indications that the religious right has pulled democracy quite far from that middle road. It also sounds like yet another Crusade has begun; Right Wing Christians and Right Wing Muslims taking over governments and enslaving people for their armies to fight for world domination. They have been perpetrating these wars and killing millions of people for over a thousand years and all supposedly for the greater honor and glory of God. Both sides comprise the largest population in Hell.

Actually, Mr. Paine, our former president, who is often times referred to as King George Bush II, indicated early on that the invasion of Iraq was a Crusade.

And the people? What did they do neighbor? Did they rise up? Did they take to the streets by the millions to protest these constitutional violations? Did the Supreme Court exercise their constitutional power by declaring that entire republican administration unconstitutional and putting the constitutional process in motion for the arrest and trial of all offenders? Did the Congress stand against these violations or did they sit meekly in fear and become complicit in this overthrow of American Democracy, thus reflecting the anti-democracy actions of the Supreme Court? The Constitution has provision for civil punishment and a process leading to prison terms for elected officials committing crimes while in office, but the exercise of valid Constitutional power requires much more than the summer soldiers and sunshine patriots that currently occupy the Congress, Presidency, and Supreme Court as well as all processes down to

the local level of each state and each
community.
.

I'm afraid that your assessment is quite accurate
and valid Mr. Paine, but is not the population to
which you refer also infected with right wing
fascists working to bring down our Democracy?

Yes neighbor, more true today than ever. Their
task is dangerously close to successful
completion.

Time passes quickly on your porch neighbor for
it is close to first light and we are not yet near
the conclusion of this topic. But I'll tarry long
enough to sit back and finish this fine brew.

We both sat back and watched as the silvery
path began its retreat toward daylight.
Time was growing short but I wanted to ask a
rather silly question.

Mr. Paine, did Benjamin Franklin actually say
that in wine there is wisdom, in beer there is
freedom, and in water there is bacteria?

He laughed loudly and took some time to
compose himself.

If he did say that, and I believe he did, it was because of an experience I had during my first crossing, sponsored by Mr. Franklin, from England to the Colonies. During my voyage, I became deathly ill, while five other good people died because of contaminated water. I was unable to leave the ship when we at last secured in port. Mr. Franklin's personal physician fetched me to his home where it took the good doctor five weeks to bring me back to reasonable health. Without Mr. Franklin's kindness and concern, I would have died in obscurity that first day.

And you went on to become known as the Father of American Democracy. Was that just coincidence or the hand of God?

He raised his cup, as did I, and finished the brew.

I don't know neighbor, but I will not deny the possibility.
Considering what is happening to democracy, does it really matter?

I suppose not.

Mr. Paine put down his cup, stood up, corked the spirit bottle, posted his three pointed hat, and stepped off the porch bidding me good morrow and indicating that he would be looking forward to our next meeting.

I was going to call after him. I had wanted to ask him if he knew that Abraham Lincoln is said to have written a defense of his Age of Reason.

But first light was quickly gaining the advantage so I decided to wait till our next meeting.

I watched after him till out of sight.

His gait remained measured and thoughtful, but he did take the time to turn and call back to me a question: Neighbor, if corporations are now people, why do they not pay taxes at the same rate as people??

Conversations with Thomas Paine

Chapter Three: Banks and Real Estate.

It's getting so that I don't have to see the changes in the moon to know that it's almost time for another conversation with Thomas Paine. But I do so enjoy the beauty of the change and those multicolored rings.

There is also a change in the air that you can feel; like a fog driven mystical energy that gradually envelopes and surrounds the senses. Everything seems to stop. No trucks or cars on the coast road, no sounds of any kind anywhere. A kind of stillness sets in and demands one's complete and undivided attention.

I stepped onto the porch at this late hour; coffee, spirits, and mugs in place, sat down and was determined not to fall asleep this time.

I was successful in staying awake and grew impatient so I walked down to the road to look at the view from the same perspective Mr. Paine had the night of our first conversation. The scene was and is magnificent. It looks as though one could almost walk up the silvery path across the water all the way to the moon.

Then from the porch behind me came: Ahoy stranger, I have an extra chair and cup if you would like to rest awhile before continuing your journey.

Thank you Mr. Paine, I believe I will accept your kindness for I am quite weary and I have a long journey yet ahead of me.

You surely do neighbor, you surely do.

I stepped onto the porch, wondering about the comment just taken, shook Mr. Paine's hand and sat opposite while he poured freshly roasted hot coffee and a good measure of spirits.

I took the warm mug in both hands, brought in the pleasant aroma, as did he, stretched out my legs and felt the fine brew warm my insides.

I'm a bit behind my time neighbor, for I tarried a bit to listen to Mr. Hamilton's perspective on the current economic crisis.

I'll get another mug if Mr. Hamilton will be joining us.

No, he will not be with us.

Mr. Hamilton doesn't get out as much as I, if at all.

Mr. Paine, I had meant to ask you if other Founding Fathers or other historically significant individuals can ever visit and join in our conversations?

No, neighbor, no visits from any others are possible.

Why not?

Because neighbor, I do not have a grave like the other Founders. I am free to roam and view the decay of democracy that was my brainchild. Both curse and blessing appear to apply.

I understand Mr. Paine and apologize for the interruption.
What did Mr. Hamilton say about all this economic fraud?

Suffice it to say that Mr. Hamilton had a great many opinions about the financial direction of these various states and none of them good. He became quite angry at times as he has been known to become. He even became embroiled in a duel at one time as you must know.

The first item he mentioned, after reminding me that if we have indeed chosen Democracy as our preferred form of government then we have a moral duty to provide all needed support, is that the word American should be stricken from AIG because there is nothing about AIG that remotely resembles America. He went as far as to say that no banking institution or any company in America qualifies to have the esteemed name of America upon it.

He indicates that the controversy over the bonuses paid to corporate criminals is a diversion dangled in front of the government and the American public to cover up what is really happening; which is that the bonuses are, in point of fact, not bonuses at all and as such any discussion related to contracts is moot because the contracts are also, in point of fact, not valid. Bonuses are bribes awarded to corporate personnel willing to commit criminal acts. They have been designed to cheat the people, their investors, and our Democratic form of government.

Contracts obtained through subversion, guile, false premise, forgery, and used for the purpose of hiding illegal movement and use of funds obtained through the use of said contract renders the instrument invalid and the individuals in breach of contract and criminal code. Business, or any entity, cannot contract around the Constitution, the law, and all regulations put in place to protect people at all levels of Federal, State, and local communities.

These funds received from their high risk customers who paid extremely high insurance premiums, the majority of which, are legally required to be held in trust to pay eventual claims. Instead, these funds have been, were and are continuing to be diverted to inside individuals for personal aggrandizement or kickbacks to customers. Mr. Hamilton suspects both arrangements and the practice of these deceptions seem to be quite prevalent throughout your insurance, banking industries, real estate, education, and corporations in general.

Really Mr. Paine, no wonder he's not happy. In other words, it's taking money from customers, using it for something else other than contractual responsibility, and hoping that new customers will provide more and enough money to keep the deception going. That's what Madoff has been doing. It's called a Ponzi scheme.

Exactly neighbor, America's entire economy appears to be a Ponzie scheme as you put it. That is exactly the game, only much larger than Madoff and includes the real estate industry. The foreclosure crisis was only the tip of the iceberg. Eventually, it will be shown that banks have also fraudulently double sold the collateral that is intended to back their loans. Collateral backs a granted loan and cannot be fooled with, which indicates the need for some type of controlled and enforced regulation. Remember, over regulation leads to loss of individual ownership and Communism and state controlled dictatorship, while too little regulation leads to Fascism and religious dictatorship.

Wait a minute Mr. Paine. Many companies, have been paying out millions, maybe billions, in so called bonuses every year for a long time. So now there's no new money to cover the old money so our government has to bail them out? Additionally, banking irregularities, along with fraudulent title companies are destroying the real estate market which was the strongest component of our economy?

Yes neighbor, a pre planned event conceived and engineered with the permission of past republican administrations in conjunction with corporations for the purpose of establishing a right wing fascist government dictatorship or breaking away and starting a new right wing country; Government flowing to the people instead of from the people.

America is supposed to be a country of laws for the protection of its citizens but these laws have not been enforced by the executive branch for years. Instead, this past President, 2000-2008, wrote hundreds of signing statements undermining the other two branches of government and even instructed his executive branch that they are not obligated to follow laws enacted by Congress; which, by the way, is a criminal breach of Federal Law.

It seems to have worked quite well for Republicans because billions of taxpayer dollars are being given to individuals and companies that took the funds needed to keep the American economy solvent and are not only, not being prosecuted but are being asked to rebuild the economy that they engineered into devastation. The game continues and power flows ever increasingly from the government to the people instead of from the people to the government as was written in the Constitution neighbor.

The same argument can be made for home mortgage contracts not being valid. The banking industry leaders devised mortgages with calculated illegal usury acceleration clauses and undisclosed hidden fees that individual citizens never had a chance to meet, engaged in forgery, switched loans; which, in turn, renders mortgage contracts invalid on a massive scale. They bundled the paper from the loans and sold them off and separated the collateral from those loans and sold it elsewhere to banks and investors all over the world. One way that the banking industry can get away from these illegal loans is through non-judicial foreclosure that leaves the Constitutional court process and due process in general out of the loop of fraud or the continuing criminal enterprise for profit. It is similar to the Red River Texas land scams of the 1800's.

Loan modification programs that do not exist are dangled in front of unsuspecting home owners for the purpose of continuing the original deception and gain further profit through the foreclosure process and erase the original illegal and illegally obtained mortgage contracts. Loan modifications that are granted are actually minor fee reductions and not modifications to the loan at all. They are called loan modifications to simply fool the so called home owner and lengthen the foreclosure process in order to charge extra fees and scavenger attorney costs.

Non Judicial foreclosure is just one option that banks have to cover up the fact that not only were the loans bundled and sold off to unsuspecting investors foreign and local but the collateral for those loans, namely the land and buildings, were separated from the loans and sold separately to other banks, foreign and local, who are hiding behind the 'trustee' structure and 'loan servicing' structure. The bank that is represented by the trustee front is the actual holder of the collateral real estate and pushes for non-judicial foreclosure in order to take possession of the property and sell it out from under the duped citizen that has been making monthly payments on what is essentially air before he finds out that his home has been stolen. In other words, the customer is paying on a loan that no longer exists because it no longer has the collateral real estate to back it up. It's also a takeoff on the old Wyoming land grabs that rich cattlemen used to steal land from homesteaders in the old west.

The initial debt went out of existence when the collateral was separated from the loans and

TILA truth and lending disclosures were violated. That is Law.

Since the customer or original purchaser was in first position relating to the real estate purchase when the first breach of contract and disclosure violation occurred they are entitled to clear title, free and clear ownership to their property, plus punitive damages. That is why when customers left title companies with their closing loan papers firmly in grasp, those loan papers were not copies of their signed documents. The purchaser is holding copies that do not show their signatures and thus are different from what the bank and title company possess. It is quite possible that the actual signed papers have information relating to the loan terms that show the fraudulent manipulation perpetrated and implemented by banks. Regardless of what Republicans say, some regulation is needed to protect citizens, non-citizens, investors, and foreign governments from illegal real estate contract manipulation within our financial institutions.

Does Mr. Hamilton have any suggestions for current home owners in financial trouble due to massive bank fraud?

After his initial well aimed blustering he recommends that home owners individually or in large groups find attorneys or groups of attorneys that will accept their cases on a contingency basis and sue mortgage holders, mortgage servicing companies, debt scavenger law firms, title companies, brokers, and especially the banks for breach of contract and disclosure violations to blunt the foreclosure process and petition the government to prosecute and enforce existing racketeering statutes. Individuals should seek reimbursement of all funds and payments paid to banks and obtain financially clear titles to their properties plus damages, not as groups, but as individuals. Class action settlements favor the banks not the cheated home owners. A large fund is needed for individuals cheated out of their properties to draw upon because judges in judicial foreclosure cases impose flat or monthly bonds payable by the defrauded home owner to protect the criminal actions of bankers engaging in the fraudulent real estate loan business. Remember, State Assemblies have given banks the fraudulent power to take people's homes without court due process allowing banks to become the defendant in these cases, mirroring illegal Administrative Law, and are granted the individual rights of individual defense. The victim is unfairly burdened with the burden of proof as a prosecutor.

Neighbor, let me say that economies, companies, education, banking or any social system cannot be built or rebuilt from the top down. They can only be rebuilt from the bottom up. To do anything else is a continued illegal use of funds.

Overall neighbor, sometime around your year 2004 the banking industry noticed that many Americans were sitting on their real estate equity, possibly saving it for their children and their own retirements. Being the corrupt offspring of the Temple money lenders that Jesus rightfully drove from the Temple, the current banking and Wall Street scavengers, with the consent and help of Republican administrations, devised methods of cheating people out of their home equity, and their homes, through loan manipulation practices after closings and applying inflated fees during foreclosures.
The real coup comes later when the banks 'forgive' the destroyed homeowners false debt and illegally report their foreclosure profits as the former homeowner's income to the internal revenue service thus forcing the homeowner to pay taxes on the bank's profit from the sale of

the homeowners property while the bank pays no tax at all. No risk to the banks at all plus they get the side benefit of getting ownership of the property which they sell at a 100% profit; the property which was supposed to be collateral for the loan. There is no such thing as forgiven debt. The collateral real estate of the homeowner secures and cancels the debt in foreclosure. Foreclosure is not income of the foreclosed upon, it is loss to be deducted. There is no tax code item number that backs this banking falsehood. The result of course is that millions of foreclosed homeowners are actually being forced into poverty while their IRS returns falsely show them as having a higher income that doesn't exist, thereby allowing right wing republicans to falsely report that middle class income is rising and that the American economy is recovering when in reality, it is not. Result: The middle class continues to shrink and the Sunday morning media morons scratch their heads and talk bipartisan democracy. I am reminded of herds of Judas goats.

As you can see by the human wreckage left in the wake of the big business real estate ship of global criminal corruption, they and all their related industries were, and are, quite successful.

They call it 'good business', instead of the global financial cannibalism that is being perpetrated against we the people.

For those homeowners who did not fall for the mortgage snake oil banking tactics, the banks devised the reverse mortgage scam to get the property away from the 'homeowner's' children after the duped 'homeowner' dies. If there is a number beyond trillions, the amount stolen from the American people lies somewhere there.

Mr. Paine, it seems, from your description, that what banks are perpetrating is not forgiveness of debt, but right wing politicians, judges and lobbyists developing a system of untaxable profit that forgives theft by bank.

Mr. Paine sipped his drink thoughtfully. What do you mean neighbor?

Lobbyists collect millions of dollars from right wing fascist individuals and corporations using the guise of non-profit status and use the funds to bribe politicians to make changes that are against democracy. In the meantime, republican governors, like the dorkinator in California, appoint right wing administrative law judges to positions as judges in Superior and District Courts, and do not allow transcripts of hearings where homeowners are applying for relief from this oppression, thus manipulating the court system away from Democracy and to the support of Right Wing Fascism.

It is simple Mr. Paine; lobbyists to politicians; politicians to judges; judges to denial of individual rights; people losing their properties to theft by bank; Democracy losing to Fascism. It's all been done before.

Wall Street and big business really jump for joy because they get to take all their contributions to right wing fascist non-profit groups manipulating Republican politicians and judges off their income tax.

As was said in Chicago during the Roaring Twenties: A good criminal organization needs politicians and judges in their pocket with a good Chicago Piano for back up. Some type of reversal of Democracy manipulation is sorely needed Mr. Paine.

Interesting and well struck neighbor. But before you can initiate the process of recovery, a nation must severely punish all who have broken the law and recover funds stolen because they are needed for the infrastructural rebuilding process and as a clear demonstration to the citizens that Democracy is continuing to work, and is working, on their behalf. Property wrongfully taken must be returned to their rightful owners and reparations paid. There are laws that exist for these situations and enforcement is required. That is Democracy.

I slowly reached over and poured us both more coffee and spirits. Then I stood up and stared blankly out over the water and just could not immediately absorb the magnitude of the criminal activity perpetrated upon the people of our democracy even though it was just expressed. Every aspect of American life is being driven downward; it's called good business and is rewarded with more than trillions of tax dollars. The manipulated government will bail out the banks but not the citizens cheated by those banks. Maybe Frank and Jesse were right about banks, and,.. whatever happened to the RICO racketeering laws?

A complete and utter lack of integrity across the entire spectrum of leadership, business, education, and human services must exist to produce this immense amount of illegal activity that has become standard operating procedure.

Mr. Paine, there simply are too many people in America that make their entire living twenty-four hours a day, seven days a week by cheating other people who live in America. The excuse that many bank employees use for committing these crimes is that they are in fear of being fired if they do not become criminals.

Also, all entities in America need to pay taxes in order to bail out America, not just everyday people.
No taxation without representation applies more today than it did in your time sir.
I believe it was President Grant that suggested the taxation of all property equally whether church or corporation.

I believe President James Garfield also weighed in by indicating that the divorce between church and state ought to be absolute. It ought to be so absolute that no church property anywhere, in any state, or in the nation, should be exempt from taxation; for if you exempt the property of any church organization , to that extent you impose a tax upon the whole community.

I can only comment neighbor that the truth continues to be self-evident.

If I may quote myself neighbor: The moral duty of a man consists in initiating the moral goodness and beneficence of God manifested in the creation towards all creatures. That seeing, as we do, the goodness of God in all men, it is an example calling upon all men to practice towards each other, and consequently that everything of persecution and revenge between man and man and everything of cruelty to animals is a violation of moral duty.

Sorry Mr. Paine, I really do not see how moral duty and God exist or are applied anywhere in today's America.

It is known as tyranny neighbor. Our government is now religion based and controlled. It illustrates the point that government and business are man-made religion centered but not God centered; the separation of God from church and the inclusion of the state with the church results in what you live today here in your time. The phalanx of the tea party must be defeated and driven from the temple of Democracy neighbor.
You have your work cut out for yourself neighbor.

Me?? What can I do? I'm just one old person, closer to the end than the beginning.

Democracy is a birth to death responsibility neighbor, remember?

Mr. Paine stood up and finished his brew with a sigh.

Well, first light is beginning to grey the night, so I must be on my way and leave you to ponder and plan. Think on the subject for a time and we will speak of it again.

Well, I do recall the words of a famous person that may apply:
One man with an idea can change the world.

Good words neighbor. I should be able to recall who said such memorable words but confess that I cannot.
Was it Washington? No, he never said that.
Franklin? No, I recall everything he said.
Jefferson, it had to be Jefferson. He was very astute at those types of observations especially over hot buttered rum with a sprig of cinnamon.

No Mr. Paine, none of them.

Well, who was it? I must be on my way but would like to know before I leave.

I slowly finished my brew before relieving Mr. Paine's curiosity.

Captain Kirk.

Conversations with Thomas Paine

Chapter Four: Holiday Meeting:
December Twenty Fourth:

Snow and cold were everywhere. It was about
that time again to meet with Mr. Paine. I
prepared in the now usual way by grinding
freshly roasted coffee beans to use as a base for
the favored brew.

I recalled that Mr. Paine had served for a time
with General Greene, so I had purchased some
good ole Southern Comfort and Malibu Rum for
possible inclusion. A choice of one was what I
had anticipated.

I went out to sweep the porch and was greeted
by Mr. Winter in very high feather with extreme
cold and excessive wind, so, with haste; I set up
the sunroom for our conversation and settled in
to enjoy the view outside from the inside this
time.

I became fascinated by what the movement of ice and snow crystals across the multicolored hue around the moon was achieving. The beautiful rings seemed to move faster and slower depending on the velocity of the wind and produced a sparkling effect akin to distant stars dancing with ever so many vibrant colors against the many sunroom windows. I was distracted and just a bit annoyed by a knock at the door and realized that I had completely forgotten that Mr. Paine would be arriving this night.

I opened the door to a surprisingly warm breeze and Mr. Paine dressed as though it were summer or at very least, late spring.

Step outside neighbor and behold an occurrence that rarely graces us.

As captivating as the view was from the sunroom, becoming part of nature's showing was many times more captivating. There was no other recourse than to lose one's breath and stand completely in awe of the beauty being provided and be grateful for the privilege. Something extremely special was happening and I really appreciated my inclusion.

How long do we have to enjoy this, Mr. Paine?

Till first light, neighbor, only to first light.

Colorful movement swirled in all directions at the whimsy of the wind but somehow demonstrated purpose of thought. The colors were so intense and many that they could not be named due to their vibrant movements, sparkling prism interactions, and to rarely ever having been seen. The mind was totally absorbed with attempting to interpret that which was being presented.

The colors seemed to form fields of intensely beautiful flowers swaying to the wind and joined imperceptivity by young girls dancing and moving in perfect time to be joined by young men dancing lovingly with them and suddenly intermingled and interrupted by sharp flashes of light which seemed to highlight the movement of troops silhouetted as dark shadows illuminated by artillery flashes which just as quickly returned to young girls moving in time among the beautiful fields meticulously placing the colorful flowers on soldier's graves with the controlling wind slowing to such an extent that the young girls gradually faded back into the intensely colorful flower fields gently and slowly swaying in the mild breeze leaving the observer completely mesmerized and altered.

What do you see neighbor?

I see mankind and their circular fascination with peace and war from the beginning of time; control of masses of people by small tyrannical special interest groups resulting in enormous profits for the few with death and destruction for the many; inequality personified. But then again I'm exactly the wrong person to ask Mr. Paine.

Why do you say that?

Because if I were one of twenty people observing the exact scenario or sequence of events, and all of us were asked to described and interpret what we observed, nineteen would match while I would see things completely different from the others.

I don't see that as a problem neighbor. Not everyone agrees on all things. I believe that I was a formerly living example of that very thing.

But I always carry it further by insisting that the other nineteen are completely wrong, which has meant that I have lost just about every position that I have ever held rather than adjust my interpretation.

I can understand that that could pose some individual problems, but would like to hear some examples before forming an opinion.

I make a point of burning every bridge behind me and I have a lifetime full of them, Mr. Paine.

Neighbor, that only means that you are an individual that is always moving forward.

Huh, never thought of it in just that way Mr. Paine.
But, to answer your question, I recall that I was watching the 2000 election. A reporter told Mr. Bush that he had just lost Florida and the camera moved in for a close up of his face. Just the look on his face for a few seconds; a look of total surprise and disbelief told me that Florida had already been stolen for the Republican count. I turned off the television and had no need to follow the rest of the coverage debacle because I knew with certainty that we would have at least eight years of further movement toward extreme Right Wing Christian Fascism with the Constitution continuing to take the usual severe

beating from the Republicans to the point of being discarded.

A great number of people, neighbor, put at risk all they had and all they and their children would ever have, with a large number over the years, providing the ultimate sacrifice in order to write down and preserve the individual rights for ALL the people that ever would live in America. American Democracy is still to this day unique. Its form of democracy is the only kind that has ever existed. To observe the Constitution being trampled underfoot by individuals born of this nation is painful in the extreme. And to have that being done in the name of God makes the entire situation much worse and exceedingly more dangerous.

Mr. Paine, I observe two major sight lines emanating from World War II, which appear to influence or connect the paths our leaders choose to follow; connecting historical dots so to speak. Two future leaders came out of that war directly opposite in view, personality and purpose.

One with a basic dislike of people, deeply Christian Quaker with an overriding drive to control the population for their 'own good' and to suppress the Constitution in order to achieve a religious controlled government to stand as a beacon against all things non-Christian. He saw himself and his chosen followers as being above the law or possibly dictating the law for the people's 'own good.'

And the other with an outgoing personality and a personal fondness for people with an overriding drive to insure that the Constitution be preserved and be all inclusive for all the people in this nation and a strong conviction of religious freedom with an understanding of the need to separate organized man-made church, not God, from government in order to avoid dictatorship. In other words, to maintain the concept of separation of church and state as written by the Founding Fathers. He saw himself and those with him as guardians of the Constitution, which is the first function of the Presidency after constitutional enforcement. He believed in Lincoln's "of the people, by the people, for the people" No Republican would ever think to say that today.

The two leaders of course were Richard Nixon and John Kennedy.

Their beliefs and personalities deeply influence the path that each political party follows in terms of how Americans live from day to day, how we do business, how we are educated or not educated and how and for what purpose we fight wars or wars for business.

Both were religious. One believed that people needed to be taken care of because they do not have the ability to make choices that are in their own best interest, so the government should be empowered to make good Christian choices for the people; a major platform of the Republican Right Wing. A dictatorship government with life controlled by religious structure, much like in the Middle East is the Republican Party goal for America.

The other understood that religious structure needed to be separate from government, as set forth by our Founding Fathers, in order for individual freedom and free will to exist and took his oath of office seriously; preserve, protect, and defend the Constitution of the United States of America. Keep God in your life, but keep his self-appointed corrupt human representatives from controlling the activities of democratic government. All great American Presidents have understood this and lived or died by it. However, they also understood that going too far to the left would also lead to state controlled dictatorship and be a mirror image of far right dictatorship except without religion.

Most, from my time, fought a long protracted war for exactly those reasons neighbor, and clearly understood that which the few great presidents have implemented and protected.

Eventually the political assassinations of President Kennedy, and later his brother Robert and then Martin Luther King blunted a natural move toward the political middle and left the path open for Nixon and the far right to pull the nation back from the middle and continue the journey toward the Christian fascism of the far right thus making the current Republican Party the party of Fascism.

The major difference between John Kennedy and Richard Nixon is:
Kennedy sent Americans out into the world to spread peace and help people build better lives for themselves and their families and provide a good example of Democracy in action.

Nixon, being corrupt, laid the path for Americans to go out into the world and spread war, death, corruption, and destruction in order to gain profits for the select few to control the American population and 'do what is best for them', thus insuring that America becomes a globally hated Fascist nation.

One could reason neighbor, that the path of corruption laid out by a criminal President Nixon and his republican fascist followers eventually led to the destruction of the Twin Towers on 911. History has taught us that the seeds that grow into such cataclysmic events are sown well before their actual occurrence. During my travels neighbor, I came across a pamphlet like paper, I believe you call them articles in something called the BBC, written by an Englishman of all people. The pamphlet indicated that some phone conversation tapes of President Lyndon Johnson show proof of the treason of Richard Nixon during the 1968 Presidential election but were only released forty years later in 2008.

I never read or heard anything about any such thing in the media Mr. Paine. What are the particulars of this paper?

It appears neighbor, that President Johnson had the South Vietnamese embassy altered by the

NSA to record all conversations taking place there. The recordings captured something called back channel communications between the campaign of then Presidential candidate Richard Nixon and the South Vietnamese Ambassador that interrupted the peace talks designed to put an end to the war. The Ambassador was informed that he would get a better deal if the peace talks could be postponed till Nixon became President.

The rest of course is history; Nixon became President, escalated the war four more years, gaining large war profits for the few while 22,000 more American soldiers died, thousands more wounded, and countless numbers of additional Vietnamese were killed, wounded, and uprooted.

The article reported that Nixon committed the criminal act of treason but Johnson caught him through the commission of a criminal act using the NSA to record the South Vietnamese Ambassador's conversations. It's not surprising that democracy is coming to an end and your Congress is gridlocked and government in general not effective. The two political parties, using the criminal acts of the other against each is resulting in polarization and the loss of Democracy.

The seeds of the current cataclysmic events of this millennium were indeed sown well prior to their actual occurrence.

Now the business plan of the Republican Party is coming to fruition. American Democracy is in danger of being virtually gone and the American people are so under educated and unknowledgeable about the Constitution and our Democracy that a valid vote is purely accidental.

It can also be reasoned neighbor that the planet would be a very different place here in your time had President Kennedy been able to carry forward his vision of America leading the way to peace throughout the world and the Twin Towers may still be standing .

Mr. Paine leaned forward in silence with his elbows on his knees; his hands clasped together and stared angrily out over the water which became strangely dark and violent.

After a time he leaned back, took in a good measure of our brew and sighed.

Neighbor, our discussion makes me recall the biblical tale of Cain and Abel. Could it be that the world has simply played that scene over and over countless times from Eden till now? Could it be that people are only divided into those two camps and all that can be attained is occupancy of one side or the other?

Where would free will and freedom fit, Mr. Paine? Into which camp? Both Left and Right extremes provide a snake oil illusion of freedom to entice unsuspecting trusting people to their respective bias.

Yes, neighbor, freedom for some in power, but not freedom for all, and that has always been the bug in the milk. Most of the population is enslaved to insure the freedom of those who have seized power and wealth; Fascist power on the Right and Communist power on the Left.

I believe that the people you call the Greatest Generation came closest to what we envisioned during my time. Democracy was attacked by the Right Wing Fascism of the Third Reich. The Greatest Generation found the right mix, counterattacked and protected freedom and equality for all. The very same ideas and ideals that led to World War Two are performing their corrupt work here again, neighbor.

I do not believe that the Tea Party Right Wing should be likened to the Nazis of the Third Reich, Mr. Paine. That really would be extreme.

The Extreme Right of the Republican Party represented by the Tea Party in no way are Nazis, neighbor. Hitler and the Third Reich made their intentions clear; announced their hatred of Democracy as outlined in Mein Kampf; controlled an entire German population with their small special interest group, took away individual rights, adjusted the courts to take people's property, and attacked nations, which resulted in the deaths of over seventy million people worldwide. Democracy is being changed from within America from Democracy to Fascism by the same Right Wing principles responsible for World War Two. The danger to Democracy is exactly the same, neighbor, and tenfold more hideous.

But the Tea Party Republicans claim to be American Patriots, Mr. Paine.

They are Patriots neighbor. The special interest Tea Party and their big money lobbyists are Patriotic American Fascists dedicated to changing our Democratic form of Government. Listen to what they say about people and compare it to what the Founding Fathers said about 'We the People'.

If what you claim is true, Mr. Paine, then what is happening in the Republican Party makes them worse than Nazis.

Exactly neighbor; think about Democracy in the same way that we, you call the Founding Fathers, presented it. After all, we did write it down for everyone that came after us.

You see neighbor, every sixty to eighty years or so since 1776, a 'Greatest Generation' has risen from within the American population to adjust the course of democracy by whatever means necessary to protect that Democracy and preserve it for all who are yet unborn. Remember neighbor, Democracy is not global. Tyranny in all its forms is this planet's global government and has been from the beginning.

Mr. Paine, this current generation call themselves the Millennials and think of themselves as the current 'Greatest Generation.' I believe they are known as the 'M' generation.

Surely you jest neighbor. I wish you could join me in my travels. You, as I, would come to unveil the truth of the current generation as the techno savy, self absorbed, self obsessed, masturbation generation. In that respect this generation is accurate and can be known as the 'M' generation.

Is that why these beautiful emotionally colorful scenes are playing out before us this night, Mr. Paine?

I never thought so before neighbor, but now I'm beginning to view these incredibly beautiful images with new eyes.

Maybe we are being shown that a third camp is required. One that is dedicated to the expansion of the middle against the Fascist Right and the Communist Left; the enhancement of the constitution; a rededication to the achieving of freedom for all and once again government by the people; a Constitutional rededication based on God endowed free will instead of man-made abusive religion. After all, the middle, and most populous in the nation, does not have a political party to represent them. Possibly bringing back the old Democratic-Republican party of Jefferson and practiced by Lincoln may be the answer to representation for all the people.

Well struck neighbor, well struck. That fits well; a new way forward by retrieving the past. The past as written by those of us you call the Founding Fathers.

The image of Thomas Jefferson and Abraham Lincoln walking side by side down the road of Democracy, with Jefferson reaching out his left hand holding back the Left and Lincoln's right hand pushing back against the Right, is most compelling. Traveling in that little space between those twin giants of freedom for the people dwells Democracy.

We both sat back and drained our mugs as the swaying colors seemed to increase their intensity.

Is this coconut I taste in this brew tonight, neighbor?

Yes it is Mr. Paine, how do you like it?

Seems to mix splendidly with the southern whisky and coffee. Yes, I like it. Thank you neighbor.

You're welcome, Mr. Paine.

Neighbor, I really stand against these wars that our country has been fighting during the past sixty some odd years of yours. There doesn't appear to be any clear definition between the winner and loser thus keeping the citizen population continually at risk and continually draining the economy and placing it at the disposal of a very few powerful individuals who lack integrity and have a strong tendency toward theft, hoarding, war profiteering, and Fascism. You call them republicans, and they do not pay taxes.

We also call them Wall Street, Big Business, One Percent, and Right Wing. Seems to me, Mr. Paine, you have already provided a clear definition of what war and peace today have become through their intermingling.

Yes, unfortunately that appears to be true neighbor. Your President Eisenhower was quite correct when he warned us to beware of the Military-industrial complex, and recall that the corrupt Nixon was his Vice President. I sometimes wonder what Mr. Eisenhower was really saying in John Kennedy's ear at President Kennedy's first inauguration.

And also recall, Mr. Paine that Bush was Nixon's Vice President.

Yes neighbor, I do recall that the baton of Nixsonian corruption has been continually handed off from then till now.
After all this passage of time, it should be quite clear universally that countries that invade other countries eventually always lose regardless of their type of government or religious affiliations. Invasion means exactly what it is; Invasion. People just do not want to be controlled by people from outside their own borders, whether invaded in the name of God and religion, Fascism, Communism, Democracy, or all of them.
An example of course is that slaves fought for the Confederacy toward the end of the Civil War which can be likened to Black individuals who join and support today's anti-democracy Republican Party.

It also sounds like entire nations interfering with one another's free will, Mr. Paine.

Exactly neighbor. Well struck again. It is the one constant that history has clearly demonstrated over and over through time immemorial. Wars are always about the denial of free will through the spread of religion, spread of political ideas, the acquisition of enormous profit for the very few and cheap labor through domination and slavery to guarantee continued profits over time. And they are always started by those very few who never actually participate in the hazardous battle campaigns. When rich people start wars, poor people die. It has been so from the beginning.

Sounds like RICO? May I fill your cup, Mr. Paine?

Absolutely…..Thank you neighbor.

I filled Mr. Paine's mug, as well as my own, and we sat back in silence to contemplate our thoughts while I tried to understand the knowledge which was attempting to reach me through these amazingly colorful intense movements and displays.

For the first time I noticed that Mr. Paine was wearing glasses and the cosmic performance being presented appeared to apparition forward to some type of intense multidimensional anguish reflected in his lenses.

I was reminded of someone screaming in frustration at the top of their lungs and beyond about things, that to them are entirely obvious, to people who either cannot hear or refuse to understand what has been presented throughout eternity over and over as being simple, honest, true concepts of everyday living, coupled with warnings of extreme danger.

A strange curiosity and admiration entirely engulfed me as I wondered how images and information of such intensity and frustration could be presented so graciously, reflecting great care, concern, and understanding; yet here it was, presented right in front of me, with ease to absorb and understand.

But the great question still remained to frustrate: What do I; we; all of us; do with it??

Mr. Paine removed his glasses and placed them carefully on the table next to his mug.

His look told me that he understood all this in life, just as clearly as he understands it now. It was now obvious to see why he was awarded the titles of 'Father of American Democracy' and 'Father of the American Revolution.'

Neighbor: Why did the giant not awaken on 911, as it did on December, 7th 1941?

What we obtain too cheap, we esteem to lightly, Mr. Paine.

You quote a fine gentleman there neighbor, but are you referring to the general lack of education, the lack of citizenship, or the corruption and political manipulation of the hoarders and hiders of the nation's wealth?

All of them Mr. Paine, and yet much more; I do not believe that people in general, no matter how they label themselves; Republicans, Democrats, or Independents; realize that the same individuals, with minor exceptions, that subverted the Constitution and stole millions of dollars under the Nixon administration are the exact same individuals that subverted the Constitution and stole billions of dollars under the first and second Bush administration's, with their getaway strategy being exactly the same in both generational time frames, thus altering the course of Democracy toward Fascism.
Or, people do understand, and they simply don't care. The Constitution was completely undermined as they pushed the country farther into Right Wing Conservative Fascism. In order

92

for them to form their new country, the United States as begun by our founding fathers, must fail either by outright destruction or by gradual evolution, as is now the case, into religious controlled Fascism. Proponents of the extreme Right consider themselves the founding fathers of their new Christian nation to be composed of the former United States as a whole or whatever part they can steal. The real struggle is a religious battle for who will control what's left of the United States; Christians or Muslims.

I drew down a good amount of our draft, placed my mug on the table, put on my glasses and in my own misplaced arrogance attempted to mirror Mr. Paine's eyeglass reflection representing my observations as being personal and newly discovered as if history had no skills of observation and interpretation. The increased intensity of the colorful presentation before us was not lost on my brain.

His small smile prior to taking in a good amount of draft immediately and gently exposed my arrogance without rebuke and I waited for the question that would right the error.

Mr. Paine poured a bit of the Malibu Rum while I in turn poured a larger than usual amount of coffee. He saw that amount, raised me with a small bump of Southern Comfort, and asked a question that I neither thought of nor anticipated thereby completely negating personal arrogance and gently bringing me back into constructive unencumbered thought and interaction.

Do you know how these false Christians were able to accomplish this multiple constitutional subversion neighbor and push us closer to their goal of Right Wing American Fascism controlling the people of these United States?

My surprise and hesitation was obvious. I smiled as I silently theorized how Mr. Paine must have enjoyed doing this to his contemporaries; directing all back to the Constitution and the rights of man.

Excuse me Mr. Paine; I have to get something in the house.

I know neighbor, it's in plain sight on your desk for ready reference use where all people wishing to protect their freedom and their children's freedom should keep it and use it daily.

I returned with my desk copy of the Constitution of the United States; sat down, took a sip of the favored brew and began to look up the answer to Mr. Paine's query.

Let's see; Article II. The Executive Branch, the President, section four; Removal of Executive and Civil Officers states that the President, Vice President and all civil officers of the United States shall be removed from office on impeachment for, and conviction of, treason, bribery, or other high crimes and misdemeanors.

That's right neighbor. First the President, Congressman, or any other civil officer, has to be impeached before they are tried and punished for criminal activities.

Yes Mr. Paine, and that impeachment trial takes place in the Senate with the Chief Justice of the Supreme Court acting as Judge as stated in Article I. Legislative Branch; Congress. Section seven: Judgment in cases of impeachment shall not extend further than removal from office, and disqualification to hold and enjoy any office of honor, trust, or profit under the United States; but, and here's the part that answers your question; be liable and subject to indictment, trial, judgment and punishment, according to the law.

That's right neighbor, by not punishing political criminals that work in our government the Constitution and our Democracy have been subverted continually since the Nixon administration and less openly, before.

When you look at it that way Mr. Paine, then Gerald Ford becomes the worst President in history next to Nixon. He pardoned Nixon and allowed Nixon's criminal personnel to continue to be employed in government and become part of the George Bush the 1st and George Bush the 2nds administrations.

Actually neighbor they and their minions worked at various times for all Republican Presidents since Nixon and continued subversive work against our Democracy and for Religious Right Wing Fascism. Remember, President Reagan spoke out of both sides of his mouth by raising taxes six out of the eight years in office and vetoed the resolution to support releasing Nelson Mandela from Prison. As you may recall, openly Racist South Africa elected a Black President well before the 'supposedly non-racist Christian United States.'
Reagan was an actor, and as such, trained to represent himself as something he was not. He opened the door wider than Ford; enough for

Banking and Wall Street Corporations to begin
taking over our Democratic Government and
changing it to tyrannical oligarchic Fascism by
using lobbyistic bribery for insertion into our
three branches of Government.

President Ford said that the country needed to
move forward and not look back. He declined to
prosecute the Republican offenders and was
lauded as a nice guy with the best interest of the
country and the American people being
foremost. He chose to ignore the sections of the
Constitution that opened the door for the
criminal prosecution of the Republican President
and his staff. He was perhaps an American
Christian Republican Fascist.

That's pretty close to what our current President
Obama has indicated about prosecutions of the
Bush administration and he's a Democrat. How
do you account for that neighbor?

Money Mr. Paine, money. A great deal of
money, especially from Wall Street, that
traditionally went to the Republican Presidential
Candidate was contributed instead to Mr.
Obama's campaign. I believe that he has stated
that there will be no prosecutions and that the
country must move forward. I think President

Obama is beginning to look a lot like President Ford or someone that the Republicans need to blame for crimes committed by the Right Wing. He is being victimized by Right Wing campaigns of discredit and is reacting by backpedaling instead of standing for the people. The decision as to what kind of President he will be is entirely in his own hands.

I believe that President Obama would do well to go down into the basement of the White House, rummage around, and find President Theodore Roosevelt's Big Stick and apply it appropriately and vigorously in defense 'of the people.'

Well struck neighbor; Presidents are elected as being either a Republican or a Democrat. Those that leave office and are still considered a Republican or a Democrat generally have been non effective, poor, corrupt, or uninspiring Presidents. They simply placed party biased loyalty above what a President actually is supposed to do. Those Presidents that based their decisions on what they honestly believed to be representative of the people and the Democracy as written by the Founding Fathers became the Great Presidents and mostly angered both sides of the political spectrum. To become a great President, the President has to evolve into something he was not when elected, namely an American President. And from our first days as a nation till now there have been too damn few of them.

Neighbor, we have been discussing Fascism in relation to your current day Republican Party. Should we not define Fascism prior to moving forward with these conversations to see if there really exists a fit to the Right Wing of the Republicans?

Sounds more than reasonable Mr. Paine, I'll get Webster's dictionary.

Daniel Webster wrote a dictionary? I thought only Jefferson did things like that.

No, Mr. Paine, this is a different Webster....I think.

Oh, I stand corrected neighbor. Please proceed.

Lets see,...Fascism; here it is: Fascism: noun: rods bound about an ax; ancient Roman symbol of authority. Sometimes F- a system of government characterized by dictatorship, belligerent nationalism, racism, and militarism. Oh, and how about sedition Mr. Paine?

Sedition: [n <L sed-, apart + itio] a stirring up of rebellion against the government.

What do think Mr. Paine, are the definitions of fascism and sedition a match to the Republican Party?

Absolutely, especially the extreme Right Wing Religious Tea Party. We appear to be tracking the Right beast neighbor.

We both sat back and took in the now almost frenzied colorful apparitional movements that were engulfing us. Then just as suddenly all slowed to a graceful approaching finale.

Mr. Paine raised his mug and touched it against mine. Here's to Freedom and Democracy; it is not over yet. I touched mine to his; here, here.

It saddened me to notice that the dark sky was just ever so slightly showing a touch of grey that signaled the approaching end of this indescribable night.

Well neighbor, I will soon have to continue my journey but will leave you with these questions about some items that you mentioned earlier.

Why did the vast majority of Muslims switch their votes to George Bush two weeks before that election? I believe that without the Muslim vote George Bush would not have been able to get the election into a Fascist leaning Supreme Court. He would have lost the popular vote by much more than he did, as well as the electoral vote, and would not have made it to the right wing supreme court to steal the election and thus would never have been President. The influence of extreme Muslims actually elected Republican George Bush to the Presidency in 2000. A year later, extreme Right Islamics performed a Pearl Harbor type attack, using airliners as delivery weapons, against New York and murdering over 3,000 American Civilians, declaring war in the process and got away with it. Coincidence? Question: Why would the Muslim general population want American Fascist Republican George Bush as President of the United States?

The ramifications of your questions Mr. Paine are extremely far reaching, but since you are stating statistical fact, it should be explained or at least presented. One month before the election the Muslim vote was split 50-50 between candidates Bush and Gore. Two weeks prior to the election the Muslim vote switched to Bush almost ninety per cent. That comprises a large swing in a very short period of time which has left many questions related as to reasons why?

The most logical reason could be the political similarities between these two political entities of the Conservative Right; Al Qaeda and our own home grown Fascist Tea Party. In General, both Muslims and Christians are right wing and not strong supporters of Democracy. Both Christians and Muslims, especially those that have slipped beyond their religious borders into fascist controlling small interest groups, live a religion based controlled life and have similar views as to religion, people, government, and women. It is difficult to imagine what the basis of all the grief and crusades was, and is, all about between them.

That question has had millions scratching their heads for more than a thousand years neighbor. No satisfaction yet.

Mr. Paine, I believe each non-Muslim individual should sit down with a Muslim and ask for a complete explanation and definition of the word infidel. These types of interactions may be quite informational.

Look at the current situation here in your world today neighbor. All over the world there are uprisings with people seeking freedom and democracy while the United States is being pushed into Fascism by a rich special interest group changing the House of Representatives into the United States House of Tyranny against its own people with a biased court system supporting their abuse of the population. The rest of the world does not like Right Wing Fascism as clearly demonstrated by the worldwide sacrifices of millions of people during World War Two.

Good points Mr. Paine. The rest of the world surely has noticed that we no longer can function as a democracy and can no longer be relied upon as a leader nation representing how well a democracy works. By allowing Right Wing extremists to change our government we have let the rest of the planet down.

Of course they have noticed neighbor, they are not stupid. The nations of the world have experienced many changes in tyrannical governments over thousands of years. They see that our media is right wing owned and controlled and that gridlock does not apply to our current political quagmire. The result, as world nations observe, is that friendly free nations no longer trust us to lead, while nations we see as enemies smell our self-inflicted weakness and move militarily in our direction going right through our former friendly allies. I believe neighbor that our current United States greatly fears the F word. It is never mentioned anywhere when discussing our current negative political changes.

Excuse me? Did you say the F word, Mr. Paine?

Yes neighbor, Fascism. Unless I am greatly mistaken, isn't Fascism and its negative effect on America what we have been discussing at length?

Oh, I thought you meant a different F word; one that is being applied toward us worldwide, especially within our own borders thanks to the Republican Party.

If I could, Mr. Paine, I would suggest giving an annual award to a Right Wing Republican politician who most represents anti democracy, racism, corruption, snake oil, sedition and treason against the United States. I would cast it as a dirty broken Liberty Bell and I would call it the Felonius Balonius Award. I believe he was an ancient evil, lying politician supporting every conceivable abuse of people.

Felonius Balonius, Neighbor? Oh, I understand it now.
Felonius, as taken from felony, and Balonius, as extracted from baloney.

Well struck neighbor, well struck. Actually, you could present the award to both Republicans and Democrats alike, as well as any number of businessmen, bankers, educators, media hacks, and corporations, but I enthusiastically point out that the award must, by sheer numbers and necessity, be awarded daily.

We both laughed, finished the favored brew and sat back to observe the finale.

Overall neighbor, The United States must not emulate Germany of the 1930's. The United States must use what happened to the population of the Germany of that time as an example of what not to become. Fascism can, and is, happening here to the population of the United States now in your time the same way as happened in Germany then as well as now.

Suddenly all movement before us simply stopped as though frozen in time with the colorful informative chorography gently fading back into the approaching light.

Remember this as I journey neighbor; Pearl Harbor was indeed a day of infamy as proclaimed by Democratic President Franklin Delano Roosevelt and the response it evoked and all that followed was proper and led to victory over worldwide right wing fascism thus saving Democracy.
911 is America's day of National disgrace. Christian Right Wing Republican President Bush just sat there and did nothing. There was, and still has been, no response to that attack. Our enemies laughed and danced in the streets and are still performing that ritual today all these years later. There are reasons why the Republicans chose to allow that infamous attack to go unanswered. Those reasons must be found, uncovered, and addressed before any hope of returning Democracy to the United States can be achieved. The answers are found in the corporate inhumanity of big business as warned by Jefferson, Lincoln, Theodore Roosevelt, Franklin Roosevelt, Dwight Eisenhower, John Kennedy, as well as many others both Democrat and Republicans of yesteryear. Their unheeded

warnings are resulting in a change of government from Democracy to Right Wing American Republican Party Christian Fascism.

What Mr. Paine? Are you saying….?

I am saying neighbor, that our enemies, no matter what they call themselves, know American History better than we the people know our history. It doesn't take a Harvard Scholar to see that all great wars were fought and won by Democratic Presidents.

Wait Mr. Paine, Abraham Lincoln was the first Republican President and he fought and won the Civil War and freed the slaves.

Neighbor, today here in your time, Lincoln would not be a Republican. He represented and spoke for the principles of the Founding Fathers. It was Republican President Theodore Roosevelt that demonstrated that the extreme right was betraying America in the years following Lincoln's assassination. President Theodore Roosevelt broke away and started his own Bull Moose Party, also known as the Progressive Party, which made it possible for Democrat Woodrow Wilson to take the White House and eventually help fight and win World War One

with that eras 'Greatest Generation.' Same
Republican betrayal, different generation.

What does that have to do with 911 Mr. Paine?

The seeds of cataclysmic events are sown well
before their actual occurrence, remember? All
events are connected neighbor.

The World Trade Center was attacked with a car
bomb during Democratic President Clinton's
Administration.
What do our enemies know about President
Clinton?
Our enemies see the picture of young Clinton
shaking hands with President John Kennedy.
President Kennedy was willing to go to nuclear
war to protect Democracy and the American
People.
The car bomb at the Twin Towers may have
been a test to see if Democratic President
Clinton would react like past Democratic
Presidents, especially President Kennedy.
President Clinton, without hesitation provided an
instant response by reaching for the arsenal of
missiles and used them instead of invasion
troops. He made our terrorist enemies flinch and
duck. His reaction confirmed to our enemies that
a Republican President needed to be in the

White House in order for an attack against America to be successful. A president that will either do nothing or eventually find a reason or manufacture a way to reach for expendable ground troops, aircraft, or costly invasions to develop business profits for a corporate community that doesn't even pay taxes to support Democracy is the confirmation our enemies search for to proceed without reprisal. Our enemies work to develop a nuclear capability and will use it against us, especially our civilians, without hesitation. Their fear is that we will develop a 'Greatest Generation' to stand against them in total war.

For now, our enemies dictate the terms of how wars are fought. The United States, or any nation, cannot win any real war unless they dictate the terms of war or must withdraw and that is not profitable. Same Republican betrayal, different generation.

President Theodore Roosevelt and his Progressives broke from the Republican Party and published a sixteen page campaign pamphlet called 'A Contract With the People.' A National Health Service to include all existing government medical agencies and Social Insurance to provide for the elderly, the unemployed, and the disabled were just two of the items promised to the American people. Now a bit more than one hundred years later, Republicans are still blocking all these help type programs for 'We the People' that Europe, Asia, and Russia have long since instituted for their people. Same Republican betrayal, different generation.

Mr. Paine stood up, as did I, shook my hand and posted his three pointed hat.
Also remember neighbor that the American people, like their Republican Fascist President who stole the Presidency through a corrupt right wing controlled Supreme Court, also sat there and did nothing.
I suggest you study the Trading with the Enemy Act; it was invoked in November, 1942 to stop bankers like Prescott Bush and Walker, founders of the Bush Family Oligarchy, from continuing to do business with Hitler. Look up all the players and their families to see where they are today and the connection to the Bush family as well as the damage being done to our American Democracy.
Study the Administrative Procedure Act of 1946 that attacks Democracy by allowing the development of cancerous judicial administrative law courts by legislating around the Constitution. It demonstrates how Democrat

McCarren and Republican Joe McCarthy
bayonetted Democracy in the back.
Look closely at the politicians, bankers and
businessmen prior to and since that time and
decide for yourself.

Walking throughout America has given rise to a
number of questions neighbor, some of which, I
would like to discuss with you at a later time:

If Mr. Lincoln freed the slaves in 1863, why was
there a need for a Civil Rights movement more
than a hundred years later? I observe throughout
this once great nation that the attitude and
feeling about Black people, as well as other
groups now like Hispanics, Native Americans,
and Asians, is about the same as it was during
my time

Why do not Religions pay taxes? As I recall, the
Constitution indicates that there shall be freedom
of Religion; not freedom from Religions paying
taxes. And what is this nonsense about non-
profit organizations? There is no such thing.
Religion and non-profits make billions of dollars
each and every year and hold trillions of dollars'
worth of property which provides vast sums of
income each year; not to mention all their

investments and corporations owned. All is taxable and needed to support our Democracy.

If Corporations are now people, as the Supreme Court and the Mormans now claim, why do they not pay taxes as a single non-married individual? Additionally, corporations should pay an employee tax for each one of their overseas employees. Republicans claim that you now live in a global economy, thus you should also have global taxation for all corporate profits. That is Democracy.

Till next time neighbor.

Till next time Mr. Paine.

Mr. Paine stepped off the porch and began his measured thoughtful gait to points unknown to me.
About half way to the coast road he turned and called to me: Wait neighbor, I forgot to give you something.

To my wonder, everything stopped. All sound, wind, movement of any kind simply ceased as Mr. Paine returned to the porch, sat down, poured himself coffee and spirits and with serious thought began to write as the dawn was held back.

I took my place opposite, poured myself a sound measure and waited with great curiosity about what was being written.

Mr. Paine, I interrupted, there is something I must ask you before you begin. Was there a Quaker Christian leader by the name of Thomas Nixon at your deathbed trying to convince you to recant your beliefs regarding the abuses of man-made religions and their leaders?

Most assuredly neighbor. He tried, as well as some Milhous people, with much enthusiasm and was soundly rebuked and rebuffed. As I recall, Nixon stormed out carrying much anger and spouting great amounts of Christian cursing, some of which, I had never heard the like of before, not even from Mr. Franklin.

What about Willett Hicks, Mr. Paine? He said you were a good man and an honest man. He was a Quaker Christian preacher and yet he stood by you and was your friend. How do you explain that?

Mr. Paine answered without looking up from his writing. Bipartisanship, neighbor, bipartisanship; one of the major ingredients for the recipe of democracy, and is seriously lacking here in your time which is a major reason why you no longer live in a democracy.

When Mr. Paine completed his task, he handed the list to me, poured a sound measure, and stretched out his legs.

He refilled my mug and asked me to read his list:
Sixteen million children in America go to sleep hungry every night. That is not Democracy.

Women in the military are being abused as well as the men in the military who stand up and try to help them. That is not Democracy.

The election of 2012 demonstrates that the feeling toward Black citizens is exactly the same as it was in my time of 1776 and before. That is not Democracy.

Administrative Law Courts remove the individual rights of the people guaranteed by the Constitution of the United States. That is not Democracy.

Banks can take away people's property without going to Court through non-judicial foreclosures. That is not Democracy.

Business entities use pension funds to make investments but, the profits are not returned to the pension funds while the losses are deducted from the pension funds thereby reducing monthly pension checks with huge bonuses being paid to criminal individuals. That is not Democracy.

Business and banks operate with no risk at all. All losses are passed on to the people while individual rights have been taken away. That is not Democracy.

The Republican Party controls and operates their own welfare system for the wealthy. Republican entitlements must end. That is not Democracy.

Politicians enjoy a Government sponsored health care program. That is not Democracy.

There are too many people who do not pay into
        Social Security. All must pay into the
        system. That is Democracy.

The Christian Right Wing Tea Party is staunchly
against Democracy and are the true illegals and
interlopers of your time. They are bribed
politicians and minions of the extremely wealthy
Christian special interests and illegally hold
sway over the Republican Party and the United
States House of Representatives. That is not
Democracy and they revel in destroying
Democracy by using the taxpayers own money.

Inequality, economic and personal, is at a higher
level that it was before and during the Great
Depression with the middle class shrinking more
than at that time. That is not Democracy.

Smaller government in a Democracy means less
Democracy.

I took in a sound measure and read aloud Mr.
Paine's list and commented:
Tea Party, Mr. Paine? No argument there.

Administrative Law Courts cancelling individual
rights and taking people's property without due
process Mr. Paine? No argument there.

Sixteen million hungry children in America has increased from twelve million hungry children in America. Could be that bad economic times have increased our hunger problem.

Neighbor: Greedy, self-centered, concentration of wealth leads to takeover by tyranny currently hiding in man-made religion, and the institution of special Courts outside the Constitution leaves all people stressed, hungry, and living under a dictatorial form of government, leading to the devaluation of human life. Hence, children go hungry, Wall Street flourishes, a chosen few become wealthy and powerful, while the people scratch for a living, provide cheap labor, fight war profiteering actions worldwide, go hungry and die without notice, nor care.

I understand, Mr. Paine, but I do not see how the plight of Black people is still the same as it was in your time and is related to the election of 2012. Even Black leaders say that Black people have come a long way since your time.

Neighbor; the election of 2012 was contested between a white Christian Bishop and a Black Scholar. The Christian Bishop repeatedly indicated that the Black candidate does not understand the complexity of economics. The Bishop's son indicated publically that he felt like slapping the Black candidate after one of their debates. Remember, the Black Presidential candidate in 2012 was the sitting President of the United States.

In my time, and before, the feeling was that Black people did not have the ability to understand anything that White people could, like reading, writing, math, complexity of economics, or anything related to everyday living and were put on earth by God to serve as slaves. In order to correct their behavior, Black people were routinely slapped daily to correct a perceived breach of behavior, and much worse, for every contrived reason by every white family member.

Racism is a learned trait, neighbor, and has been passed from generation to generation here since the 1600's, not to mention the rest of the world for thousands of years.

Yes, Black people have come a long way, but many White people have not, and now here in your time, Black people, White people, and the largest segment of the American population, the so called Middle Class made up of racial and ethnic groups rooted worldwide, is being forced away from their last chance Democracy. After Mr. Obama was elected President of the United

States, the republicans stated their one and only goal was to get Obama out of the White House, thus ignoring our Democracy and all representation of the people. That, sir, is Racism with a capital R and one of the major ingredients of Fascism.

Everything in this world for all time has always, boiled down to profit for the few by suppression in order to achieve cheap labor, which can only be attained through oppression and slavery. The most disturbing aspect of the whole discourse is that not one American of any race or ethnicity stood up neighbor.

Mr. Paine, I believe that women in the military and the men that try to help them are being seriously abused. If the 'Band of Brothers' still exists, then would not each unit member band together and protect the unit members that are being abused?

Good point neighbor, good point. The infrastructure of the military has changed to reflect the non-representation attitudes of business leaders, church leaders, and our politicians. Zeros, as you refer to them. Some of our volunteer soldiers and officers even take pictures of themselves proudly standing under the Waffen SS insignia of Nazi Germany.

Republican Party Welfare system for the wealthy Mr. Paine? I do not understand that one. Republican entitlements for the wealthy?

Republicans are against helping poor people in any way and deride financial aid, food stamps, health care, and education for the less fortunate. Yet they champion farm subsidies for wealthy farmers and ranchers, and enormous tax breaks for big business and Wall Street, while sixteen million American children are hungry.

As far as Social Security is concerned, many people, like teachers, do not pay into Social Security Mr. Paine.

Exactly neighbor, Social Security was originated for all the people and is the basis for pension and Medicare health care for seniors. Therefore Social Security needs to be paid into first by all the people and if people want other pension plans in addition then they are free to sign up for those, otherwise the Social Security continues to be depleted out of existence, which is a major platform of your current Right Wing Fascist Tea Party Republicans.

Government sponsored health care for politicians? I do not think I see that one either, Mr. Paine.

Neither does the rest of the country neighbor. Politicians pay nothing for health care nor the medical attention, hospitalizations, tests, doctors and everything related to their own health. Everything medical for politicians is paid for by the government with taxpayer money, while the American people are scammed with corporate snake oil and told to like it.
Politicians, democrat and republican, and their families have a health care system for themselves based entirely on Socialism, yet they stand staunchly against sharing any part of their health care program with the people of America who they are supposed to represent and protect.

Inequality at an all time high, Mr. Paine? I believe you are correct and our time here is a reflection of the past especially the inequality of the late 1920's and the 1930's depression.

Neighbor, it is a mirror image of that time. Recall again the strong rise of Fascism during that time and now here in your time Fascism is strongly rising beyond the economic depression and middle class destruction of that time. Here in your time Democracy does not dwell.

Mr. Paine, I have never really connected all these items before.

Remember this on your journey, neighbor, After a law is passed and adjudged Constitutional by the Supreme Court, the President cannot participate in changes or modifications to that law and Congress cannot ask the President to negotiate all or any part of that passed and approved law. All individuals residing in this nation are required to abide by that and any passed law, including the President and politicians of all persuasions, regardless of the number of bribes doled out by lobbyists.
It then becomes the sole job of Congress to do their jobs, as assigned by their oath of office and the Constitution to debate and legislate new laws to cover any majority perceived deficiencies regarding all passed laws. Majority rules neighbor, not individual districts trying to extort power.
The President is not a legislator or member of the Congressional Branch of Government. He cannot negotiate on a law passed by Congress, but he is the chief law enforcement officer of this nation has been given the responsibility and

power by the Constitution to arrest, detain, and prosecute any individual, including Congressmen and former Presidents, refusing to obey any law that has been passed by both houses of Congress and adjudged as Constitutional by the Supreme Court of these United States.

Each branch of government is required by oath to do their Constitutionally assigned and accepted jobs. Politicians cannot violate their spoken oath without penalty and may not contract around the Constitution or any law as is currently being done at the local, state, and federal levels.

Checks and balances neighbor, checks and balances. Abide by them or lose them neighbor.

As I said neighbor, you have your work cut out for you. Study the list that grows each day and all we have discussed and we will continue our meetings to search for more solutions that allow a return to Democracy.

I wonder, neighbor, if I might be able to find Button as I travel?

Oh, and don't forget about 2016 neighbor.

Yes Mr. Paine, the Presidential election. I will not forget to vote.

That's hardly an historical event of import neighbor, especially with the American people voting in favor of Right Wing Fascism.
I am speaking of the copyright on Mein Kampf expiring in Bavaria in 2016. Every Right Wing global tyrant is going to be slopping that garbage around again as confirmation of their racist and political bias and using it for its original intent; the destruction of Democracy.

With that, Mr. Paine raised his mug and said: Democracy and Liberty for ALL this time.

I raised my mug and replied: Here's to us and those like us; damn few of us left.

I matched his toast with great confusion and with many silent questions while we both stood and finished our draft.

Mr. Paine placed his mug on the table, shook my hand, sighed, smiled, posted his three pointed hat, and stepped off the porch to continue his quest. As he reached the road, he turned, removed his hat and raised his hand. Remember this as your journey continues neighbor: Banks, corporations, insurance companies, politicians, church leaders, school districts, and all manner of current corruption forcing tyranny upon the population will learn, as history has demonstrated clearly so many times, that when people lose their freedom, they will rise on stepping stones of their dead selves to regain it.

Merry Christmas Neighbor, Merry Christmas.

I smiled sadly, and with a strange inner peace, took notice that the dawn was now released to continue its advance against the grey retreat of darkness. I returned Mr. Paine's parting wave and curiously wondered what path Mr. Paine was attempting to set myself, and all of us, upon.

Gradually, I began to become quite tired and everything began to move toward a foggy apparitional reality.

I attempted to return Mr. Paine's seasonal farewell.
Merry Christmas Mr. Paine, Merry Christmas.

Mr. Paine heard neighbor's farewell as he crossed the coast road.
Thomas Paine turned back for a parting wave and could see only wilderness where the house had stood.

Coming in Book 2:

Thomas Paine journeys toward bloody frozen Valley Forge with George Washington and the Continental Army; searches for neighbor; continues writing the Crisis Pamphlet Series; and moves closer to the founding of Democracy and the United States of America.